DECOLONIZING AFRICAN HISTORY

Toyin Falola

DECOLONIZING AFRICAN HISTORY

Carl Schlettwein Lecture 15
Basler Afrika Bibliographien

The Basler Afrika Bibliographien is part of the Carl Schlettwein Foundation

Cover image: Class room scene in Bamako. This picture was created
in the framework of the project Longing for the Future at the Centre
for African Studies Basel (photographer: Zoumana Sidibe, 2015).
Editors: Pius Vögele, Henri-Michel Yéré, Veit Arlt
Layout and typesetting: Tilo Richter
ISBN 978-3-906927-50-3
ISSN 2297–7058

FOREWORD

Toyin Falola—in the field of African History this name is simply unavoidable. From my own humble beginnings as a student in the field to the present day, the name and the person have been omnipresent. Indeed, Falola has been described as "probably the most prolific and wide-ranging historian of Nigeria in the world".

I hasten to add that this description does not necessarily do justice to the range of his interests, in the sense that his scholarship has reached well beyond the borders of his home country Nigeria to engage with the Atlantic world, with the Americas, amongst other spaces. Falola is the author or editor of nearly 120 books. No less than five volumes of Festschriften have been published in his honour and the University of Ibadan in Nigeria has named one of its annual conferences after him—The Toyin Falola Annual Conference.

Such recognition from the University of Ibadan must feel special for a Nigerian historian: not just because of being acknowledged in one's city of birth—but also because this University has been the cradle of Nigeria's first and foremost school of historiography. Simply known as the Ibadan School and spearheaded by the likes of Kenneth Onwuka Dike, Jacob Festus Ade Ajayi, this is the school in which Falola's writing has been anchored. The Ibadan School is marked by a concern to recount a history that centre-stages African initiative and influence on the unfolding of African affairs. It did so by displaying a range of innovative methods, most notably in its use of oral sources, and in its invitation to other disciplines, such as archaeology or social anthropology, to supply their tools to the quest for an unbroken African historical narrative.

The reach of the Ibadan School in Nigeria was such that completing his BA and in 1981 a PhD at the University of Ife, today known as Obafemi Awolowo University, did not shield Falola from its effects. Ten years later, he joined the University of Texas at Austin, which has since become his academic home.

One of the hallmarks of Falola's impressive scholarship is his capacity to bring in new and refreshing perspectives to topics that were thought of as well-worn subjects.

Let me present two examples: one example could be the topic of violence in the colonial context, in which Falola managed to bring in nuanced perspectives as to why, in the case of colonial Nigeria, some chiefs and kings resorted themselves to violence, not just as an act of "resistance" to colonialism, but as a means to assert their own power, within their own polities. Statements of this kind have on more than one occasion brought about controversy—controversy we have come to understand as being a necessary part of the exercise of being a scholar.

Another example could be Falola writing a History of Nigeria, together with Matthew Heaton, in which he produces an accessible national history; a national history that is not written in a teleological way. He succeeds in historicizing the nation without naturalising it. Teleology and naturalising are precisely the most common traps in which we historians fall when it comes to recounting national accounts indeed.

The theme of the Carl Schlettwein Lecture 2022 is one dear to Toyin Falola's heart, that is decolonizing African history. In a way, it could be said of his scholarship that it saw itself as a decolonized one before the term was reprised these past years to characterise several attempts at questioning power in its many shapes and forms. It has long been important to this great scholar that African history be primarily a topic in which Africans labour in, on an equal and collegial basis with their colleagues based in universities outside the continent. On the following pages, Falola develops his views on the meaning of the term decolonizing in the context of African history and historiography.

Henri-Michel Yéré

DECOLONIZING AFRICAN HISTORY

INTRODUCTION: ORIGIN AND NATURE

"Let it be admitted from the onset that European brains, capital, and energy have not been, and never will be, expended in developing the resources of Africa from motives of pure philanthropy that Europe is in Africa for the mutual benefit of her industrial classes, and of the native races in their progress to a higher plane; that the benefit can be made reciprocal, and that it is the aim and desire of civilized administration to fulfil this dual mandate."[1]

These words from Frederick Lugard, first Governor-General of colonial Nigeria, attempted to justify a British colonialism that pursued economic interests. Britain's need for an economic advantage was the primary driver of its colonization efforts in Africa; the desire to "civilize" the continent's inhabitants was a much less urgent motive.[2] The British Empire needed raw materials to fuel its capitalist competition in Europe, and it needed foreign markets that could purchase its finished products. These requirements influenced British activity far more than any philanthropic desire to assist with African development.[3]

Africa's colonial history has clearly established that the continent's development and progress was of little concern to its colonizers. At best, these were secondary effects arising from the economic pursuit of European prosperity.[4] The provision of education, healthcare, basic amenities, and other drivers of Africa's economic and social progress were never the primary function of colonial governments. Instead, these responsibilities were taken on by different missionaries, which encouraged the proliferation of Christianity in Africa.[5]

When colonial governments took an interest in developmental necessities, they were focused either on boosting administrative efficiency or meeting the economic needs of European imperialists. The British administration's interest in healthcare was mainly restricted to services for colonial officials and their subordinates.[6] Physical infrastructure was created to access natural resources in Africa's remote regions.[7] Colonial policies for education were designed to create employable Africans that could serve subordinate roles within their bureaucratic systems. These patterns of engagement permeated every colonial activity.[8]

Europe's exploitative interest in Africa prevailed during and after the colonial period. Cultural imperialism and hegemony, as aspects of colonialism, introduced radical changes to Africa's inhabitants; the consistent imposition of foreign cultural norms had detrimental effects on traditional ways of life.[9] Even after territorial colonialism ended, the cankerworms of cultural and ideological colonialism continued to pervade the fabric of African societies and their values.[10] The civilizing mandate invoked by Lugard transformed into a colonialism that endured long beyond the colonial period—its effects remain visible in contemporary African society.

Decolonization in the present day must address issues that go beyond territorial invasion and the imposition of colonial rule. It must also end colonial efforts to establish a Eurocentric civilization on the continent. Contemporary discussions of Africa's decolonization stress the need to dismantle colonial and neo-colonial dominance within political, intellectual, and economic thought processes that have long been dominated by Eurocentrism.[11] Decolonization of African history, from the post-1960 era, has been a scholarly imperative to rid Africans of colonialist falsehoods that imply African inadequacy. It has required a total reconstruction of African history from an African perspective.[12] colonialist, Eurocentric mindsets have spent decades exerting undue influence over the portrayal and perception of Africans in global society.

The decolonial concept is a contextual attempt to purge African history of Eurocentric traditions depicting Africa as a continent without heart, history, or culture. These efforts to present Africa as a "Dark Continent" gave a pretext to Europeans who introduced their own concept of illumination.[13] Eurocentrism has erroneously traced the origins, mythical conceptions, and cultural adaptations of Africa to encounters with Europeans, which ignores African accounts of African history.[14] Efforts to decolonize African history are attempts to replicate Afrocentrism and Pan-Africanism in the history curricula, strengthening an African epistemology that produces societal ideology.[15]

Scholarship has attempted to eradicate the subjugation of African perception—an act that was enabled by the abomination of the trans-Atlantic slave trade and the

European effrontery of territorial conquests and colonization—that reduced African images to inconsequentiality. Decolonization mitigates the imposition of colonial rule that replaced African systems, conditioning African minds to reconstruct their developmental ability without colonial influence. The European agenda influenced Africa's knowledge systems, reconstructed how education was acquired, and re-created colonial and Eurocentric supremacy within educational and academic materials.[16]

Notable efforts have been made to counter the pervasive colonialist misinterpretation of Africa and African history. Pan-African and Afrocentric conceptual awakenings have been propelled and reinvigorated by the diasporic efforts of Africans challenging the false supremacy of European perspectives. These individuals have highlighted the remarkable contributions that Africans have made to global development, renewing the motivation to oppose racial discrimination and liberate Africa from colonial rule. Pan-Africanist culture has worked towards the post-colonial decolonization of Africa by shunning neo-colonialist attitudes.[17]

African historians, scholars, novelists, activists, and opinion leaders—including writers like Ade Ajayi, Kenneth Dike, and Thandika Mkandawire—have defined and narrated African history with a multidisciplinary approach that is rooted in African perspectives and understandings. In decolonizing African history, their ideology has drawn from African epistemology, theories, and conceptualizations to narrate the continent's history. It has led scholars and Africans more generally to demonstrate the African potential and their ability to surmount obstacles.

The colonizers initially restructured African mindsets through the educational systems established by Christian missionaries; these schools were the initial sites of cultural and ideological infusion.[18] European missionaries, anthropologists, and tourists counducted an unimaginable invasion of the cosmological, axiological, aesthetic, and epistemological views of Africans. Colonizing forces persistently attacked conceptions of African capability and vilified allegedly inferior African traits.[19] This work was primarily conducted through education and academic teaching, encouraging students to un-learn African culture and embrace the so-called civilization of Europeans.[20] This Eurocentric mindset infected African educational systems and constrained the scope of African history, although contemporary African historians have accepted responsibility for decolonizing their academic fields.[21]

Historical African precedents and antecedents endured persistent efforts to deny and distort reality while colonizers re-scripted African history from a perspective of weakness, crudeness, and underdevelopment.[22] The response to these efforts has been a "historiography of self-assertion," which is evident in the works of Kwame Nkrumah, Leopold Senghor, Casely Hayford, and Nnamdi Azikiwe, among others.[23] This work to restore a more accurate definition of history was supported by the "historiography of decolonization," seen in the works of Jean Suaret, Kenneth Dike, Adu Boahen, Basil Davidson, Joseph Ki-Zerbo, Bethwell Ogot, Alione Diop, and others who worked to challenge colonial accounts of African history.[24]

To salvage Africa's history, a deliberate decolonization process must occur in every political and structural institution that was built on Eurocentric foundations.[25] This extends beyond academic studies of African history to systematically baptize every African institution in the reality of decolonization.[26] A coordinated effort must lay foundations for development to undertake practical projects that are sensitive to the specific needs of Africans and sustainable enough to endure through time. To advance the cause of African independence and decolonization is to involve Africa in global, ideological discussions challenging the dominance of European and North American interests in international spaces.[27] To successfully dethrone the controlling interests in international space, Africa and its Africanization process must be strong enough to withstand economic, political, and structural challenges leveled at African endeavors.

It is attractive to discuss the process of decolonization for Africa and African history, but there is the distinct possibility that it could become merely a utopian ideology that exists only in theory, remaining distant from reality. Some scholars believe that those holding the torch of decolonization are steeped in Western culture and "soiled" by the European configuration of their ideologies. The legitimacy of such antagonism is questionable, because such efforts oppose the system that created them and forged their ideas of nationalism.[28] The initial red flag of potential compromise calls the motives of early Pan-Africanists into question—these used their European education to cast doubt on whether they pursued personal goals or actively worked to reposition Africa. Such assumptions, supported by the history of early nationalists and their close relationships with white colonizers, cannot be discarded; these concerns may be as much of an impediment to current decolonization efforts as they were to past struggles.

To contend with power, one must wield power. If Africa must position itself in a global system where the fates of countries are decided by self-determinism and the exercise of strength to contend with European and North American domination, then the African continent must be suitably prepared.[29] However, intellectual and practical struggles to decolonize the continent are often diminished by the imbalance of economic resources and unequal relationships with established nations that control international bodies and institutions.[30] African countries and economies have wallowed in debt to such institutions and the European powers that influence them, which has led to constricting agreements that alter Africa's economic policies.[31] These agreements have warped other sectors and actors that would normally maintain the pillars of African society, distracting African governments from investing in the decolonization of their continent. African leaders have been prevented from empowering their educational sector to develop effective tools for promoting Africanism.

Skepticism over the decolonization of African history is strengthened by low support and voter turnout that militates against the progress of the ideology. Political institutions have failed to support this endeavor, and

African scholars have been reluctant to commit to the process. Without the support of such scholars and institutions, the general awareness of such efforts is weakened. The educational level of the continent also accounts for the slow pace of decolonization; the concept is inconceivable to those who are largely non-literate.

JUSTIFICATIONS FOR DECOLONIZING AFRICAN HISTORY

Why decolonize? Are the vanguards for decolonizing African history harboring lofty and unnecessary dreams? In fact, the dream to decolonize the continent and its history should be shared by every African. The question is how many institutions, systems, and historical accounts are completely Afrocentric, without the veneer of inferiority that colonizers imposed on African society and history.[32] Can we say that our process of conceptualization—our descriptions of ourselves, our cultures, and our epistemology—are independent of European and North American mental constructs?[33]

We cannot give affirmative answers to these questions, and as a Yoruba maxim says, *"Omo ale lo man fi owo osi juwe ile baba e"* (Only a bastard points to his/her father's house with his/her left hand). Such gestures are unacceptable to the Yoruba people, and we cannot afford to keep describing the continent from an outsider's vantage point. Such efforts are a direct admission of brain drain and an insult to Africa's intelligentsia.

Colonization itself is a concept that conditions the systems and cultures of the colonized to revere colonizers in an attitude that is similar to mental slavery.[34] Slavery is unacceptable, and the existence of colonialism in any segment of African society, and especially in its history, must be purged. African society and its history must be completely independent.[35] This is achievable if there is widespread agreement with the idea, and if conscious efforts are made to decolonize African history.

Africa has suffered from debilitating and nebulous historical derogations for a large part of its history.[36] Global powers did not initially admit that the people of Africa were human and capable of cognition. Africans were dismissed as lesser humans who were barely more intelligent than animals. This inordinate, deranged conception of the continent justified its exploitation and the enslavement of its people. An expansive slave trade was conducted for hundreds of years, abducting strong men and women that could have developed their societies on multiple fronts. And Africans could not fight or resist this depredation.[37] When the lords of the Global North officially ended enslavement, Africans became slaves under the yoke of colonialism that eroded the continent's cultural values. At that point also, Africa could not fight.[38]

In addition to these experiences, Africa has been exposed to a double standard of European scholarship and cultural judgment applying nothing but derogatory adjectives. Africa had been condemned as a "dark continent," and its residents were dismissed as lacking the cognitive ability to adequately recount their own history.[39] This behavior was supported by colonial historiography and spread by over-reaching, Eurocentric literature from "respected" thinkers in every field of inquiry.[40] This included sciences and social sciences that disparaged

African knowledge and history, even when such ideas were inarguably valid.[41]

Although the African people could not defend their continent from the disrespect of slavery and the denigration of colonialism, which were supported by lethal colonial supremacy, Africans should be able to defend themselves and their values from neo-colonialists. The present-day decolonization of Africa and African history—work performed in the disciplines of history, philosophy, and other social sciences—provides weapons that are necessary for the intellectual battles that must be waged to dismantle a colonial supremacy that disrespectfully tramples Africa's hallowed history and heritage.[42] The decolonization of African history is the only way to correct the intentional distortion of African history, revealing the capacity of the African continent and its true role in the development of Europe and America.

Can a nation develop beyond its initial levels of education, knowledge, and research? Present conceptions of development are mostly linked with the practicability of an entity's knowledge system, which means that views of African development are always framed within European conceptualizations of development, which reduces the African continent's potential.[43] Contemporary Africans choose ideas from abroad to be applied domestically. The decolonization of African history allows Africa to rediscover its original body of knowledge, restoring the continent's original education systems and embracing their unique attributes. If industrial revolutions and related discoveries were independently possible in Europe, then Africa has its own discoveries to make.

THE OBJECTIVES OF DECOLONIZING
AFRICAN HISTORY

African history can present itself to the world in the way that it wants to be perceived. It is a narrative of the past, the present capabilities, and the potential future for the entire continent. It can present the curriculum vitae of the continent's core attributes in their authentic states.[44] In the past, this summary of Africa has largely been expressed from an outsider's standpoint[45]—for this reason, the objective of decolonizing African history is to provide an intellectual approach for re-Africanizing the sterilized history of Africa and correcting the flawed narratives of the past.[46] The goal in decolonizing African history is to make Africa the primary source of information for its own narratives, enthroning the Pan-Africanist narratives without prejudice.

The basic objective of decolonizing African history has never changed. It has always involved the goal of salvaging knowledge acquisition in Africa, which includes an inward look at African methods of generating knowledge. The Africanization of history embraces African uniqueness and the specific features of history that can liberate the continent from its shackles of dependence on colonial and Euro-American explanations.[47]

To truly liberate African knowledge, there must be a conscious effort to decolonize the production and acquisition of African knowledge. This includes the reliance on thought processes and patterns that are drawn and designed from African experiences and realities.[48] To do this, all African bodies of cultural knowledge must be treated as relevant, and the prominence of traditional sources of history must be taken as sacrosanct. Sources that include oral traditions, Kebra Nagast, *Ta'rikh al-Sūdān, Kilwa Chronicle, Gonja Chronicle, Kano Chronicle,* Afro-Islamic Ajami Library, *Ta'rikh al-Fattash,* griot library, and the Afro-Christian library must be prioritized in the re-narration of African history.[49]

The decolonization of African history cannot be attained without epistemologically conceptualizing Africa's concerns about academic knowledge production and acquisition across the continent. This requires a reconditioning of the academic mindset, abandoning the over-reliance on Western models and patterns of perception that put Africans in the back seat. African issues can no longer be viewed solely through Western lenses. The decolonization of academic and educational systems and institutions in Africa would constitute a fundamental step toward recirculating an original and Africanized knowledge of African history.[50]

To confidently assert that the decolonization of African history is either in progress or has been achieved, the social fabric of African communities must be washed clean of colonial legacies that have endured through history—whether those legacies have remained unchanged since their creation or whether they have evolved into neo-colonial forms.[51] African countries must be able to assert independence, fortify their sovereignty, invest in their own economic development, create political systems that are specific to African history, and respect the core values and rights of all humans.

The dream of decolonization is not merely the agenda of a single nation; it is a goal shared by all of Africa. Such development would ensure national independence, especially in the contemporary era of globalization, and it requires shared beliefs and coordinated efforts from the continent as a whole. This includes assistance from Africans in the diaspora, after they identify and subscribe to a common destiny. In essence, it requires contributions from the African Union; New International Economic Order; New Partnership for African Development; regional organizations, such as the Economic Community of West Africa; and intercontinental bodies that subscribe to the same Pan-Africanist beliefs. They should work to concretise these developmental strategies and focus their attention on the Africanization of African history.[52]

African societies must shed their colonial skins to control the future accounts of African history. Although history is recorded in context, it must account for societal details without falsehood. Historical accounts always note and account for the nature of societal institutions in their contemporary states.[53] This means that when colonial legacies are evident in the establishment and operation of institutions, they are automatically recorded in history; the continuing operation of those institutions means that colonialism continues to determine the scope of African history. When those institutions have been decolonized, the recording of African history would be largely decolonized; the content could no longer support colonial perspectives.

Africa's progress toward full decolonization depends on a developmental strategy that releases the continent from its neo-colonial entanglements—freeing itself from the "colonial matrix of power." The neo-colonial system cloaks familiar victimizers in the guise of humanitarians racing to aid needy countries, which reinforces colonial conditioning in the developmental progress and policies of these countries.[54] This cunning deceptiveness is not limited to structural aid that bolsters colonial inheritances; it also extends to ideological orientation and conceptualization that affects accounts of African history. To break free from this continual embarrassment, which always lurks near Africa's borders, local leaders must distance themselves from lopsided international economic aid packages tied to Bretton Woods institutions that influence African decisions.[55]

Africans must act collectively to explore every available option for partnership.[56] The continent can form strong alliances with historical allies from the Global South, including Latin American states that share our colonial history—they also struggle against the forces of neo-colonialism. In order for this developmental strategy to work, the continent must also develop internal alliances to build strength on all fronts, exploring regional economic collaborations like ECOWAS, the East African Community, the Community of Sahel-Saharan States, ECCAS, COMESA, SADC, and AMU. These collaborations enable effective strategies that retain their focus on Africa's developmental independence.[57]

APPROACHES TO DECOLONIZING
AFRICAN HISTORY

Discussions began in 1960 to liberate Africa from colonialism and neo-colonialism. In the present day, we still gather to discuss these same issues.[58] Colonial influences in African history have been a multi-headed hydra, and individual achievements feel like little more than pyrrhic victories. The very fact that these discussions continue is evidence that Africa and African history are still under the influence of colonialism. The anticipated decolonization is not yet complete, and progress has been slow.[59] However, it is clear that decolonization of African history, and its subsequent Africanization, require a coordinated effort from the entire continent. Everyone must be aware that more than words are required; it needs a comprehensive effort that applies strategic methodology and unified approaches.

Research, academic scholarship, historical writings, and other accounts are conducted based on the values and needs of individual societies.[60] Regardless of the lines of logic and deduction that are applied in these efforts, their processes and methodologies will reflect their societies and their predominant values. This shows the importance of Africanizing research, scholarship, history, and literature that has customarily been developed through Eurocentric and colonial methodologies.[61] The effort to decolonize these endeavours can only be pursued by African societies that encourage and create institutions to influence the continent's written cultures. The duty to decolonize African history is chiefly borne by African writers—their views are windows for the world to access

African philosophies and worldviews. Writers, researchers, historians, and scholars must not only possess but also encourage the desire to tell African stories of African experiences, providing the imagery that represents the continent.

The Africanization of African history depends on the continent's societal orientations. It requires the involvement of every African institution that can nurture Africans with the seeds of Africanization, completely changing their perspectives on specific African experiences.[62] The continent should be ready to experiment with huge changes—like changing the black robes of lawyers to African alternatives, constructing African governmental systems that are unique to the continent, adapting local languages to provide alternatives for every foreign word, increasing the use of African languages in teaching contexts, and re-introducing African cultures to every aspect of society. This will involve a revolutionary and radical overhaul of existing societal structures. Where society goes, so goes history. The decolonization of institutions and systems in society is the decolonization of history itself.

Euro-American writers shifted the goal posts of historical relevance by stating that "history begins when men begin to write" and "without writing and so without history."[63] Written culture was slow to permeate every part of Africa in its early stages, which put Africa at a disadvantage in historiography. Early historians largely believed that Africa's past and history could not be well established by historians. Instead, the work was done by anthropologists and archaeologists who subjected the

narration of historical evidence to colonial and Eurocentric influences and understandings.[64] These European
constraints have been ideological limitations placed on
African history; they must be opposed if African history
is to be completely decolonized.

Oral traditions and indigenous historical sources have
been a rich source of information for African historiography, and they serve as a remarkable rebuttal to colonial
objections.[65] Kenneth Dike realized this importance and
explored these sources to unambiguously state that African history is as respectable and credible as any other histories. In his doctoral dissertation, he asserted that a reliance on African methodologies is neither misleading nor
less important.[66] Oral traditions preserve the rich African
past in customs, ceremonies, and rituals that have sur-
vived through time. They serve as reliable tools for the
reconstruction of an African history that supports a Pan-
Africanist outlook.[67] Dike's success in demonstrating the
reliability of oral traditions for African history has drawn
considerable value from non-written sources. It has created a workable methodology for the full decolonization
of history.[68]

Oral tradition provides a method of restoring balance
to history by providing an alternative to written accounts
that received undue emphasis—written accounts are
grounded in unbalanced conceptions that monopolize the
historical record.[69] Oral tradition has armed Africans
with additional choices for their sources of their history,
and those choices provide clear access to the facts and
myths that compose the continent's history.[70] By pairing
oral tradition with written evidence to examine the

sources of African history, the work of decolonization receives additional tools and techniques.

The intellectual communities of African societies are the primary actors in decolonization efforts; their expressions and works serve as ambassadors for Africa itself.[71] The enthronement of Eurocentrism and colonial supremacy was achieved by European intellectuals and historians who swept the world's history clean with Eurocentric brooms. They have eagerly justified imperialist escapades that have undermined other cultures ever since the fifteenth century. These intellectuals spent years transforming world history with their wands of scientific theory, elevating Europe and disparaging Africa by excusing centuries of atrocity with the label of civilization.

Intellectual hostility has been institutionalized by agencies with distorted literature, syllabi, curricula, and knowledge systems in a broader effort to misrepresent Africa and other parts of the world.[72] These colonial institutions and agencies have been localized in the form of schools that shape how knowledge is acquired in Africa.[73] When these schools were introduced to Africa, the missionaries and other educators claimed that African ideologies and educational systems were riddled with shortcomings. Africans were given no alternative to the European narratives that were presented as superior.[74] Present-day syllabi, literature, and curricula still bear the ideals of European supremacy within their texts.[75]

Educational systems, running through every aspect of society, are the threads that weave African communities into a cohesive fabric. If their foundation is destroyed, what will be left of the sectors that were largely built on knowledge acquired from such "schools"?[76] This is why decolonization requires a multidisciplinary, interdisciplinary approach to rebuild African historiography—every area of study was built on the same educational systems. Historians must be able to approach decolonization from disciplines like law, economy, linguistics, anthropology, botany, archaeology, and sociology, and other areas of inquiry that are essential for Africa.[77] Multidisciplinary and interdisciplinary attempts at decolonization do not imply that individual historians must possess detailed knowledge from every field—they can consult with professionals from these areas, although basic knowledge in a broad range of topics is desirable.

Dike's example is the first multidisciplinary approach to historiography in Africa; it laid the foundation for such interdisciplinary modes of study in Africa. Dike interpreted historical periods through two disciplines, examining the interplay of nineteenth-century European economic and political activity in the Niger Delta.[78] He evaluated socio-economic interchanges with a fusion of economics and history, arriving at an analytical methodology that formed the basis of "economic history."[79]

Cross-disciplinary institutions have given historians access to varying and diverse sources for holistically studying the African past in its original state. The Institute of African Studies in the University of Ibadan—which was established as early as 1962[80]—and the Department of Antiquities, the National Archives, and the Nigerian Institute for International Affairs were some of the institutions that served as reliable sources of information. They preserved official government correspodence and gazettes, academic and public records, and multidisciplinary materials for a holistic restructuring of African history.[81] The materials and information in these repositories have largely been responsible for the success that interdisciplinary approaches have had in decolonizing African history.

The decolonization of African history can also be approached through the introduction of centrally subscribed themes that form a trajectory for historians, researchers, and African literatures. When forces assemble to wage war, they agree on their strategy and disposition to exploit strengths and mitigate weaknesses. A similar analogy is appropriate for the decolonization of African history; similar trajectories are necessary across the continent and within the diaspora. Widespread efforts must be contributed to the decolonization enterprise across the continent, made by writers and governmental institutions that can make aggressive progress towards the decolonization of Africa and African history. Collective themes can be identified to direct intellectual progression and constructively tackle aspects of African history for overhaul and reconstruction. These themes could be adjusted annually or biannually. A collective intellectual front would enable more research and historiography from a greater number of individuals who conceptualize, deconceptualize, construct, deconstruct, and Africanize history.

Societal development naturally translates to developments in historical research, because research can only draw its momentum from society. The decolonization of

African history is not possible in an underdeveloped African society. Political institutions must be salvaged from the instability that has blocked them from taking progressive action. The African economy must galvanize towards independence and sustainability, and more widespread education should allow more people to understand these concepts—society must be positioned to deliver an independent outlook for the sake of history.

Approaches to decolonization must track contemporary developments and conditions in African communities, including the advent of social media that has spread across the world.[82] Social media has defeated distance to create fast, cheap, and comfortable avenues for communication that enable the global acquisition and diffusion of knowledge. Roughly half of the world's population is active on social media.[83] Facebook, WhatsApp, Instagram, YouTube, and Twitter account for more than 7 billion cumulative global users.[84] Cultures and social outlooks can be shared and spread across the world with a series of online posts. There are more than 500 million internet users in Africa, and 154 million of them are in Nigeria alone.[85] The rapidly increasing numbers of social media users in Africa defy any attempt to predict their future growth.[86]

Social media has enabled the contemporary ideological globalization of Africa, and it has become an important part of African societies.[87] It has been a viable tool for social change across the continent, assisting revolutions and agitations that shape African societies with campaigns like #EndSARS and the Le Balai Citoyen's condemnation of President Blaise Compaoré's unconstitutional conspiracy to extend his tenure.[88] Other efforts include the Ça Suffit movement in Burkina Faso, the Bring Back Our Girls agitations in Nigeria, and other global campaigns that incited change in African societies.[89] Social media has even toppled governments in Tunisia and Egypt.[90]

The modern invention of social media has served as a multipurpose tool, and decolonization efforts cannot ignore the importance of these platforms. The African population must be educated through these platforms with campaigns, ads, and continuous orientation to reshape the ideology of Africans and the world's perception of the continent. Efforts should ensure that these platforms consider the unique attributes of the continent and its people, cultures, systems, and values to inform their ethics and modes of operation. Africanization must be brought to social media with a determination to promote African content and originality in lieu of the Euro-American aesthetic that has saturated local societies.

INSTITUTIONS AND FRAMEWORKS FOR DECOLONIZING AFRICAN HISTORY

The colonization of every African was not accomplished simultaneously. It happened individually, and decolonization must pursue an opposing strategy. To combat colonialism, African countries must join together and chart a course for the complete liberation of African minds. The decolonization process has already commenced, with established African facilities and institutions that are ready to grow into their roles as torchbearers for the ambition of decolonization.

The creation and maintenance of African National Archives has provided a wide range of materials and information for reconstructing African history.[91] The Nigerian National Archives and counterparts in other African states have served as a major repository of colonial knowledge, containing records of colonial transactions and correspondence.[92] Towards the end of colonialism, archivists located, collected, and preserved colonial records to retain valuable details about the operation of colonialism in Africa. These archives continue to provide accounts of the colonial governments that managed the continent, divided Africa's history into discrete periods, and erased African influences. They provide records of Africa's colonization, and they reveal the extent to which decolonization must go.

National Archives across the continent—and their rich historical materials—hold significant roles in the decolonization of African history. However, they are not regularly updated with post-colonial materials. Colonization has diffused into African systems so thoroughly that it has become part of the public subconsciousness.[93] African history did not stop after the attainment of independence, and the inactivity of these archives in post-colonial periods is a worrisome state that threatens African history.

A strategic framework for decolonizing African history can be seen in the development of different regional and international research programs that created research collaborations and journals. These include the *International Journal of African and Asian Studies, Transactions of the Historical Society of Ghana, The Journal of African History, Journal of Historical Society of Nigeria (JHSN),* and *Afrika*

Zamani: an annual journal of African history. These collaborations and partnerships have become contemporary research practices through modern programs that include the African Humanities Program (AHP), International Higher Education and Strategic Projects (IHESP), and the Council for the Development of Social Science Research in Africa (CODESRIA), and many others that support decolonization structures.

Research partnerships and programs have established themes to explore major historical issues that affect the continent, retelling the African past in order to remove its Eurocentric influences. They have also supported academic inquiries through providing grants and other monetary support, enabling researchers and historians to explore areas of interest. This work towards decolonization has ensured the wide circulation of research by publishing volumes of material across the entire continent.

Despite their initial role in Africa's colonization, universities and colleges have also served as early avenues for the decolonization of African history.[94] Evidence of this contentious journey can be found in 1970, under circumstances that are specific to South Africa.[95] Due to its experiences with colonialism and apartheid, South Africa continues to struggle with decolonizing its educational institutions and establishing a constructive Africanist outlook.[96] Although South Africa's situation is unique, every African country struggles with the Africanization of knowledge formation, acquisition, and dissemination.[97] African universities and institutions are still developing complete methodologies for supporting and emphasizing Pan-Africanism.

Early engagements with the Africanization of history have their roots in the universities and colleges of Ghana and Nigeria in 1948.[98] These institutions served as an avenue for raising the flags of decolonization, setting the pace for producing African knowledge, and supporting Pan-Africanism. They served as the vanguard for the construction and reconstruction of African literature—the intellectual gladiators that surged forth from their gates bore torches of knowledge onward across the continent.

The colonial government and missionaries during the colonial era were solely interested in using education to reduce the burden of administration, training Africans as semi-professionals to work as civil servants for the government or as laymen supporting local ministries.[99] Education was part of the colonial government's developmental strategy to teach science, engineering, medicine, law, and other topics that were relevant for the colonial blueprint. In post-colonial Africa, educated individuals created colonial and post-colonial narratives of African history. Education has remained important for the continent's developmental necessities, and many African governments—especially in sub-Saharan Africa—commit about 10 to 25 percent of their budgets to education, with a substantial portion allocated to institutions of higher learning.

At University College, Ibadan (UCI), the Department of History solidified African historiography through detailed teachings and studies that earned a notable position in Africa's history.[100] Early products and professors from this department formed the Ibadan School of History, which took up an Africanistic methodology and began viewing Africa from the lenses of Africans.[101] Kenneth Dike, widely referred to as father of modern African history, led the department in establishing the Historical Society of Nigeria (HSN). As a professional body, HSN focused on coordinated historical enquiries within Africa,[102] founding the *Tarikh* and creating other internationally reputable journals that have repositioned African history. The HSN and similar bodies have widened the scope of intellectual inquiry through partnerships that include a coordinated effort with the Historical Society of Ghana.

The relevance of educational systems, universities, and colleges in decolonizing Africa and its history remains evident in contemporary society. Decolonizing African universities to promote African realities and values is *conditio sine qua non* for the decolonization of African history.[103] Unfortunately, this decolonization has not been widely attained in these institutions; curricula, epistemologies, and teaching techniques still bear the marks of colonialism.[104] Personnel within these institutions may have acquired an Africanistic outlook, but it is not reflected in their teaching or their subject matters, which leaves large numbers of people ensnared in subconscious colonial traps. The rigid academic traditions of many African universities have discouraged Afrocentric sensitivity and left them incapable of providing African solutions to African problems. Universities remain adept at producing Westernized individuals from Westernized institutions within Africa.

If African history is to be decolonized, then universities and other institutions of learning must see the need for the Africanization of their academic systems. They must create incentives to portray Africa in an African manner. This would signal that the continent is intellectually ready for historical decolonization.

Universities are essential for creating African perceptions of history, and the antiquities departments have already demonstrated their remarkable importance for the decolonization of African history. These departments have preserved ancient materials and artistic expressions from past centuries. Their efforts to protect works of art and other materials provide ancient sources of information for reconstructing previously ignored and distorted African history. Such departments are responsible for creating images and realities from African pasts and help restoring a priceless heritage.

BENEFITS OF DECOLONIZING AFRICAN HISTORY

Many problems militate against the African continent, ranging from poverty to political instability, which raises the question of how the decolonization of African history is a contemporary concern. What are the benefits of discussing and attaining such decolonization in the present moment?

The decolonization of African history allows African governments to see the continent's true nature. By providing new perspectives from different angles of potentiality, decolonization encourages further independence for crafting effective developmental blueprints. It shows how the African past can offer magnificent solutions to contemporary problems by drawing inspiration from the continent's true history. Decolonization provides a muse for looking inwards and facing our most challenging problems, supported by belief in traditional processes.

Histories define specific groups, and the decolonization of African history would allow a rediscovery of African identity—Africans could position themselves effectively on the international stage. This African identity can be salvaged from colonial trappings without seeking colonial approval. Decolonization provides space to break the chains that bind African minds, allowing them to reach their own objectives without artificial limitations. The African identity recovered from this endeavor would result in a readiness to identify structures for research and knowledge acquisition that abandon the double standards of colonial methodologies.

Africans are not lazy people, despite Eurocentric assertions to the contrary. The work of decolonization is an opportunity for Africans to demonstrate the truth, helping the world understand their great contributions and how they have assisted with global development. Modern society is more volatile than ever, and different segments are susceptible to rapid changes and disruptive cultural substitutions. The thorough projection of globalization has contributed to cultural diffusion, imposing new views and perspectives that everyone is expected to embrace.

Even the recent past has been presented as strange and ambiguous, replaced by more refined updates and developments. However, society has become more astute than it was just a few years ago; the gap of change is closing.[105] We should not be surprised by global occurrences—change is inevitable. The quick acceptance of change largely comes from people whose attitude consists of asking "what next" and "where next" instead of "where have we come from," and that explains their complacency in abandoning historical values and structures. Changes are viable, inevitable, and necessary, but they should not be an easy way to subsume African cultural values. We must neither forget the relevance of African history nor cease our demands for its decolonization.

There is no time to waste if decolonization is to outrun the relentless pace of globalization. The decolonization of African history can infuse Africanist consciousness into every aspect of change, transforming globalization from Africanist and Pan-Africanist perspectives. Decolonization cannot stop change, but it can shape and localize changes to make them suitable for African antecedents, circumstances, and world views. To seize these benefits, African history must be completely decolonized. Africans must not complement the destructive agenda of neo-colonization with an acceptance of globalization that amounts to cultural suicide.

Decolonizing African history means demystifying the African past and rescuing it from a fog of inability fabricated by the desperate Eurocentricity of colonial writers and historians. Decolonization will demonstrate the continent's true potential, offering antecedents that can drive major developments and place Africans on equal footing with "developed" nations. The fruits of decolonization will uncover and access African solutions to address African problems, serving as a bank of knowledge and resources that leaders can rely on to shape effective policies and decisions. The decolonization of history offers a true way to understand the real nature of the African people, using African lenses for identifying authentic approaches and interactions. It allows everyone to find sure footing, regardless of how many historical values they have forgotten.

CONCLUSION

History may seem abstract, but it is as concrete as the daily activities that move a society into the future. The decolonization of a society is the decolonization of its history, and the decolonization of history is the decolonization of a society. If African societies are to be freed from the rot of colonialism that has eaten deep into their fabric, then history must be decolonized in order to expose areas of focus and effective courses of action. Decolonization will restore our societal identities and create a new intellectual campaign to spur its independent development.

When a society is decolonized, it changes the recorded accounts of history and sets itself on a decolonized path. The future will be influenced by the decolonization that affects historians and the histories they write. But to attain comprehensive decolonization, the work must begin immediately. Without fully committing to this solemn endeavor, the African continent cannot shed the yoke of its colonial past!

ENDNOTES

1   Frederick Lugard, *The Dual Mandate in British Tropical Africa* (Edinburgh: William Blackwood and Sons, 1922).

2   Stanley Diamond and Eric Wolf, *In Search of the Primitive: A Critique of Civilization* (London: Routledge, 2017).

3   Hussein Bulhan, "Stages of Colonialism in Africa: From Occupation of Land to Occupation of Being," *Journal of Social and Political Psychology* 3, no. 1 (2015): 239–256.

4   Dare Arowolo, "The Effects of Western Civilisation and Culture on Africa," *Afro Asian Journal of Social Sciences* 1, no. 1 (2010): 1–13.

5   Emmanuel A. Ayandele, *Missionary Impact on Modern Nigeria, 1842–1914* (London: Longmans, 1966).

6   Mario J. Azevedo, *Historical Perspectives on the State of Health and Health Systems in Africa (Volume I): The Pre-Colonial and Colonial Eras* (Cham, Switzerland: Palgrave Macmillan, 2017), 183–214.

7   Adeoye Adeyemo Babatunde, "Colonial Transport System in Africa: Motives, Challenges and Impact," *African Journal of History and Archaeology* 4, no. 1 (2019): 14–26.

8   Benjamin N. Lawrance, Emily Lynn Osborn and Richard L. Roberts, eds., *Intermediaries, Interpreters, and Clerks: African Employees in the Making of Colonial Africa* (Madison: University of Wisconsin Press, 2006).

9   Chris Gosden and Chantal Knowles, *Collecting Colonialism: Material Culture and Colonial Change* (London: Routledge, 2020).

10   Guy Martin, "Africa and the Ideology of Eurafrica: Neo-Colonialism or Pan-Africanism?" *Journal of Modern African Studies* 20, no. 2 (1982): 221–238.

11   N. I. Vysotskaia and Arlo Schultz, "The Struggle of the African Peoples against Neocolonialism," *International Journal of Politics* 6, no. 4 (1976-77): 12–49.

12   Frederick Cooper, "Conflict and Connection: Rethinking Colonial African History," *American Historical Review* 99, no. 5 (1994): 1516–1545.

13   Jonathan Musere, *Africa: The Dark Continent According to Foreigners* (Los Angeles: Ariko Publications, 2016).

14   George A. Barton, *Semitic and Hamitic Origins: Social and Religious* (Philadephia: University of Pennsylvania Press, 1934).

15   Ronald W. Walters, *Pan Africanism in the African Diaspora: An Analysis of Modern Afrocentric Political Movements* (Detroit: Wayne State University Press, 1997).

16   Sabelo J. Ndlovu-Gatsheni, *Epistemic Freedom in Africa: Deprovincialization and Decolonization* (London: Routledge, 2018).

17   Martin, "Africa and the Ideology of Eurafrica," 221–238.

18   Ayandele, *Missionary Impact on Modern Nigeria*.

19   Kwame Botwe-Asamoah, *Kwame Nkrumah's Politico-Cultural Thought and Politics: An African-Centered Paradigm for the Second Phase of the African Revolution* (London: Routledge, 2013).

20   Botwe-Asamoah, *Kwame Nkrumah's Politico-Cultural Thought*.

21   Cooper, "Conflict and Connection," 1516–1545.

22   Cooper, "Conflict and Connection," 1516–1545.

23   Richard Rathbone, "Cultured Nations-Self-Assertion and Brokerage," in Pailo Fernando de Moraes Farias and Karin Barber, eds., *Early Cultural Nationalism in West Africa* (Birmingham: University of Birmingham, 1990).

24   Isaiah A. Negedu and Solomon O. Ojomah, "Deconstructing African History from Western Historicism," *Alternation* 23, no. 1 (2018): 302–325.

25   Esperanza Brizuela-García, "The History of Africanization and the Africanization of History," *History in Africa* 33 (2006): 85–100.

26   Richard C. Crook, "Decolonization, the Colonial State, and Chieftaincy in the Gold Coast," *African Affairs* 85, no. 338 (1986): 75–106.

27   Sabelo J. Ndlovu Gatsheni, "Decoloniality as the Future of Africa," *History Compass* 13, no. 10 (2015): 485–496.

28   Toyin Falola, *Nationalism and African Intellectuals* (New York: University Rochester Press, 2004).

29   Ian Taylor and Paul Williams, *Africa in International Politics: External Involvement on the Continent* (London: Routledge, 2004).

30   Richard E. Bissell and Michael S. Radu, eds., *Africa in the Post-Decolonization Era* (New Jersey: Transaction Books, 1984).

31   Edward Shizha, "Are we There Yet? Theorizing a Decolonizing Science Education for Development in Africa," in Ali A. Abdied, *Decolonizing Philosophies of Education.* (Rotterdam: Sense Publishers, 2012), 163–176.

32   Fred G. Burke, "Public Administration in Africa: The Legacy of Inherited Colonial Institutions," *Journal of Comparative Administration* 1, no. 3 (1969): 345–378.

33   Ndlovu-Gatsheni, *Epistemic Freedom in Africa*. See also Oyeronke Oyewumi, "Conceptualizing Gender: Eurocentric Foundations of Feminist Concepts and the Challenge of African Epistemologies," in Signe Anfred, Bibi Bakare-Yusuf, Edward W. Kisiang'ani, Desiree Lewis, Oyeronke Oyewumi and Filomina C. Steady, eds., *African Gender Scholarship: Concepts, Methodologies and Paradigms,* (Senegal: CODESRIA, 2004): 1–8.

34   Leonie Pihama and Jenny Lee-Morgan, "Colonization, Education, and Indigenous Peoples," in Elizabeth Ann Mckinley and Linda Tuhiwai

Smith, eds., *Handbook of Indigenous Education* (Senegal: CODESRIA, 2019), 19–27.

35 Madeleine Dobie, *Trading Places: Colonization and Slavery in Eighteenth-Century French Culture* (New York: Cornell University Press, 2010).

36 Noah R. Bassil, "The Roots of Afropessimism: The British Invention of the 'Dark Continent,'" *Critical Arts* 25, no. 3 (2011): 377–396.

37 Stephen Small, "Slavery, Colonialism and their Legacy in the Eurocentric University," *Human Architecture: Journal of the Sociology of Self-Knowledge* 10, no. 1 (2012): 69–80.

38 Martin A. Klein, *Slavery and Colonial Rule in French West Africa* (Cambridge: Cambridge University Press, 1998).

38 Charles Allen, *Tales from the Dark Continent: Images of British Colonial Africa in the Twentieth Century* (London: Little, Brown, 2015).

40 Joseph Conrad, *Heart of Darkness* (London: Penguin Books, 2007).

41 Teshale Tibebu, *Hegel and the Third World: The Making of Eurocentrism in World History* (New York: Syracuse University Press, 2011).

42 Andrew W. M. Smith, "Pan-Africanism and Decolonization: Between the Universal and the Particular," in Reiland Rabaka, ed., *Routledge Handbook of Pan-Africanism,* (London: Routledge, 2020), 112–124.

43 Chidozie Chukwuokolo, "Afrocentrism or Eurocentrism: The Dilemma of African Development," *Ogirisi: A New Journal of African Studies* 6 (2009): 24–39.

44 Eric Hobsbawm, "From Social History to the History of Society," *Daedalus* 100, no. 1 (1971): 20–45.

45 Basil Davidson, *The Black Man's Burden: Africa and the Curse of the Nation-State* (New York: Times Books/Random House, 1992).

46 Brizuela-Garcia, The History of Africanization, 85–100.

47 Toyin Falola and Christian Jennings, eds., *Africanizing Knowledge: African Studies Across the Disciplines* (London: Routledge, 2017).

48 Falola and Jennings, *Africanizing Knowledge.*

49 Toyin Falola and Christian Jennings, eds., *Sources and Methods in African History: Spoken, Written, Unearthed* (Rochester: University of Rochester Press, 2003).

50 Jonathan Mswazie and Tapiwa Mudyahoto, "Africanizing the Curriculum: An Adaptive Framework for Reforming African Education Systems," *Journal of Emerging Trends in Educational Research and Policy Studies* 4, no. 1 (2013): 170–177.

51 Merima Ali, Odd-Helge Fjeldstad, Boqian Jiang and Abdulaziz B. Shifa, "Colonial Legacy, State-Building and the Salience of Ethnicity in Sub-Saharan Africa," *The Economic Journal* 129, no. 619 (2019): 1048–1081.

52 Johannes Tsheola, "Trade Regionalism, Decolonization-Bordering and the New Partnership for Africa's Development," *China-USA Business Review* 11, no. 8 (2012): 1051–1068.

53 Oscar Handlin, *Truth in History* (London: Routledge, 2018).

54 Mohammed Sarwar Alam, "Illusion, Deception and Dehumanization: Neocolonial Reinforcement of Colonial Legacy and the Role of English," *IIUC Studies* 7 (2012): 55–62.

55 Anzetse Were, *Debt Trap? Chinese Loans and Africa's Development Options* (Johannesburg: South African Institute of International Affairs, 2018), 3–12.

56 Tsheola, "Trade Regionalism, Decolonization-Bordering."

57 Mordechai Tamarkin, *The Making of Zimbabwe: Decolonization in Regional and International Politics* (London: Routledge, 2012).

58 David Birmingham, *The Decolonization of Africa* (London: Routledge, 2008).

59 Birmingham, *The Decolonization of Africa.*

60 Richard Owen, Phil Macnaghten and Jack Stilgoe, "Responsible Research and Innovation: From Science in Society to Science for Society, with Society," *Science and Public Policy* 39, no. 6 (2012): 751–760.

61 Falola and Jennings, *Africanizing Knowledge.*

62 Stephanie Decker, "Postcolonial Transitions in Africa: Decolonization in West Africa and Present Day South Africa," *Journal of Management Studies* 47, no. 5 (2010): 791–813.

63 Kenneth Onwuka Dike, "African History Twenty-Five Years Ago and Today," *Journal of the Historical Society of Nigeria* 10, no. 3 (1980): 13–22.

64 Mpalive-Hangson Msiska and Paul Hyland, *Writing and Africa* (London: Routledge, 2017).

65 Jan Vansina, *Oral Tradition: A Study in Historical Methodology* (London: Heinemann Educational Books, 1968).

66 B. E. Awortu and Uebari Samuel N-Ue, "African Intellectual Revolution in the 20th Century: A Review of Kenneth Onwuka Dike's Contributions to African History," *International Journal of African and Asian Studies* 13 (2015): 140–148.

67 Daniel F. McCall, *Africa in Time-Perspective, A Discussion of Historical Reconstruction from Unwritten Sources* (New York: Oxford University Press, 1969).

68 Awortu and N-Ue, "African Intellectual Revolution."

69 Paul T. Zeleza, *Banishing the Silences: Towards the Globalization of African History* (Maputo: CODESRIA, 2005).

70 David William Cohen, "The Undefining of Oral Tradition," *Ethnohistory* 36, no. 1 (1989): 9–18.

71 Jonathon L. Earle, *African Intellectual History and Historiography* (Oxford: Oxford Research Encyclopedia of African History, 2018).

72 John Wansbrough, "The Decolonization of North African History," *The Journal of African History* 9, no. 4 (1968): 643–650.

73 Philip Altbach, "Servitude of the Mind? Education, Dependency, and Neocolonialism," *Teachers College Record* 79, no. 2 (1977): 187–204.

74 Nicholas Harrison, *Our Civilizing Mission: The Lessons of Colonial Education* (Liverpool: Liverpool University Press, 2019).

75 Kingsley Banya, "Illiteracy, Colonial Legacy and Education: The Case of Modern Sierra Leone," *Comparative Education* 29, no. 2 (1993): 159–170.

76 David Baker, *The Schooled Society: The Educational Transformation of Global Culture* (Redwood City: Stanford University Press, 2014).

77 Richard M. Juang and Noelle Morrissette, eds., *Africa and the Americas: Culture, Politics, and History: A Multidisciplinary Encyclopedia*, Vol. 1 (Santa Barbara ABC-CLIO, 2008).

78 Kenneth Dike, *Trade and Politics in the Niger Delta, 1830–1885: An Introduction to the Economic and Political History of Nigeria* (Westport: Greenwood Press, 1981).

79 Awortu and N-Ue, "African Intellectual Revolution," 142.

80 Adiele Afigbo, "The Institute of African Studies," *Africa Spectrum* 6, no. 3 (1971): 89–92.

81 Boniface I. Obichere, "The Contribution of African Scholars and Teachers to African Studies, 1955–1975," *African Issues* 6, no. 2–3 (1976): 27–32.

82 José van Dijck, *The Culture of Connectivity: A Critical History of Social Media* (Oxford: Oxford University Press, 2013).

83 Andrew Perrin, "Social Media Usage," *Pew Research Center* 125 (2015): 52–68.

84 Statista, "Most Popular Social Networks Worldwide as of January 2022, Ranked by Number of Monthly Active Users," *Statista Research Department*, accessed May 1, 2022, https://www.statista.com/statistics/272014/global-social-networks-ranked-by-number-of-users/.

85 Joseph Johnson, "Africa: Number of Internet Users in Selected Countries 2020," *Statista*, May 25, 2021, https://www.statista.com/statistics/262966/number-of-internet-users-in-selected-countries/.

86 Andre-Michel Essoungou, "A Social Media Boom Begins in Africa," *Africa Renewal* 24, no. 4 (2010): 3–4.

87 S. Ibi Ajayi, "Globalization and Africa: What Africa Needs to do to Benefit from Globalization," *Finance & Development* 38, no. 4 (2001): 6–8.

88 Christian Sturm and Hossam Amer, "The Effects of (Social) Media on Revolutions—Perspectives from Egypt and the Arab Spring," in

Masaaki Kurosu, ed., *Human-Computer Interaction: Users and Contexts of Use* (Berlin: Springer, 2013), 352–358.

89 Mourdoukoutas Eleni, "The Hashtag Revolution Gaining Ground," *Africa Renewal, United Nations,* accessed May 2, 2020, https://www.un.org/africarenewal/magazine/april-2018-july-2018/hashtag-revolution-gaining-ground.

90 Sturm and Amer, "The Effects of (Social) Media on Revolutions," 352–358.

91 Jordanna Bailkin, "Where Did the Empire Go? Archives and Decolonization in Britain," *The American Historical Review* 120, no. 3 (2015): 884–899.

92 Folashade Yusuf, "The Role of Archives in National Development: National Archives of Nigerian Perspective," *International Journal of Economic Development Research and Investment* 4, no. 2 (2013): 19–24.

93 Simon Heap, "The Nigerian National Archives, Ibadan: An Introduction for Users and a Summary of Holdings," *History in Africa* 18 (1991): 159–172.

94 Emnet Tadesse Woldegiorgis and Martin Doevenspeck, "The Changing Role of Higher Education in Africa: A Historical Reflection," *Higher Education Studies* 3, no. 6 (2013): 35–45.

95 Savo Heleta, "Decolonizing Knowledge in South Africa: Dismantling the 'Pedagogy of Big Lies,'" *Ufahamu: A Journal of African Studies* 40, no. 2 (2018): 47–65.

96 David Macfarlane, "UCT in War over 'Bantu Education,'" *Mail & Guardian,* March 11, 2011, https://mg.co.za/article/2011-03-11-uct-in-war-over-bantu-education/.

97 Isaac A. Kamola, "Pursuing Excellence in a 'World-Class African University': The Mamdani Affair and the Politics of Global Higher Education," *Journal of Higher Education in Africa* 9, no. 1–2 (2011): 147–168.

98 Tim Livsey, "The University Age: Development and Decolonisation in Nigeria, 1930 to 1966" (PhD Diss., Birkbeck College, University of London, 2014).

99 Aaron Windel, "British Colonial Education in Africa: Policy and Practice in the Era of Trusteeship," *History Compass* 7, no. 1 (2009): 1–21.

100 John D. Omer-Cooper, "The Contribution of the University of Ibadan to the Spread of the Study and Teaching of African History within Africa," *Journal of the Historical Society of Nigeria* 10, no. 3 (1980): 23–31.

101 Olutayo C. Adesina, "Teaching History in Twentieth-Century Nigeria: The Challenges of Change," *History in Africa* 33 (2006): 17–37.

102 Jacob F. Ade Ajayi "Towards a More Enduring Sense of History: A Tribute to K. O. Dike' Former President, Historical Society of

Nigeria on Behalf of the Historical Society of Nigeria," *Journal of the Historical Society of Nigeria* 12, no. 3/4 (1984): 1–3.

103 Achille Joseph Mbembe, "Decolonizing the University: New Directions," *Arts and Humanities in Higher Education* 15, no. 1 (2016): 29–45.

104 Francis B. Nyamnjoh, "Decolonizing the University in Africa," *Oxford Research Encyclopedia of Politics,* July 29, 2019, https://oxfordre.com/politics/view/10.1093/acrefore/9780190228637.001.0001/acrefore-9780190228637-e-717.

105 Andrew Osehi Enaifoghe, "The Decolonization of African Education and History," *African Renaissance* (1744-2532) 16, no. 1 (2019): 61–84.

REFERENCES

Adesina, Olutayo C. "Teaching History in Twentieth-Century Nigeria: The Challenges of Change," *History in Africa* 33 (2006): 17–37.

Afigbo, Adiele. "The Institute of African Studies," *Africa Spectrum* 6, no. 3 (1971): 89–92.

Ajayi, Jacob F. Ade. "'Towards a More Enduring Sense of History: A Tribute to K. O. Dike' Former President, Historical Society of Nigeria on Behalf of the Historical Society of Nigeria," *Journal of the Historical Society of Nigeria* 12, no. 3/4 (1984): 1–3.

Ajayi, S. Ibi. "Globalization and Africa: What Africa Needs to Do to Benefit from Globalization," *Finance & Development* 38, no. 4 (2001): 6–8.

Alam, Mohammed Sarwar. "Illusion, Deception and Dehumanization: Neocolonial Reinforcement of Colonial Legacy and the Role of English," *IIUC Studies* 7 (2012): 55–62.

Ali, Merima, Odd-Helge Fjeldstad, Boqian Jiang and Abdulaziz B. Shifa. "Colonial Legacy, State-Building and the Salience of Ethnicity in Sub-Saharan Africa," *The Economic Journal* 129, no. 619 (2019): 1048–1081.

Allen, Charles. *Tales from the Dark Continent: Images of British Colonial Africa in the Twentieth Century* (London: Little, Brown, 2015).

Altbach, Philip. "Servitude of the Mind? Education, Dependency, and Neocolonialism," *Teachers College Record* 79, no. 2 (1977): 187–204.

Arowolo, Dare. "The Effects of Western Civilisation and Culture on Africa," *Afro Asian Journal of Social Sciences* 1, no. 1 (2010): 1–13.

Awortu, B. E. and Uebari Samuel N-Ue. "African Intellectual Revolution in the 20th Century: A Review of Kenneth Onwuka Dike's Contributions to African History," *International Journal of African and Asian Studies* 13 (2015): 140–148.

Ayandele, Emmanuel A. *Missionary Impact on Modern Nigeria, 1842–1914* (London: Longmans, 1966).

Azevedo, Mario J. *Historical Perspectives on the State of Health and Health Systems in Africa (Volume I): The Pre-Colonial and Colonial Eras* (Cham, Switzerland: Palgrave Macmillan, 2017), 183–214.

Babatunde, Adeoye Adeyemo. "Colonial Transport System in Africa: Motives, Challenges and Impact," *African Journal of History and Archaeology* 4, no. 1 (2019): 14–26.

Bailkin, Jordanna. "Where Did the Empire Go? Archives and Decolonization in Britain," *The American Historical Review* 120, no. 3 (2015): 884–899.

Baker, David. *The Schooled Society: The Educational Transformation of Global Culture* (Redwood City: Stanford University Press, 2014).

Banya, Kingsley. "Illiteracy, Colonial Legacy and Education: The Case of Modern Sierra Leone," *Comparative Education* 29, no. 2 (1993): 159–170.

Barton, George A. *Semitic and Hamitic Origins: Social and Religious* (Philadelphia: University of Pennsylvania Press, 1934).

Bassil, Noah R. "The Roots of Afropessimism: The British Invention of the 'Dark Continent,'" *Critical Arts* 25, no. 3 (2011): 377–396.

Birmingham, David. *The Decolonization of Africa* (London: Routledge, 2008).

Bissell, Richard E. and Michael S. Radu, eds. *Africa in the Post-Decolonization Era* (New Jersey: Transaction Books, 1984).

Botwe-Asamoah, Kwame. *Kwame Nkrumah's Politico-Cultural Thought and Politics: An African-Centered Paradigm for the Second Phase of the African Revolution* (London: Routledge, 2013).

Brizuela-García, Esperanza. "The History of Africanization and the Africanization of History," *History in Africa* 33 (2006): 85–100.

Bulhan, Hussein. "Stages of Colonialism in Africa: From Occupation of Land to Occupation of Being," *Journal of Social and Political Psychology* 3, no. 1 (2015): 239–256.

Burke, Fred G. "Public Administration in Africa: The Legacy of Inherited Colonial Institutions," *Journal of Comparative Administration* 1, no. 3 (1969): 345–378.

Chukwuokolo, Chidozie. "Afrocentrism or Eurocentrism: The Dilemma of African Development," *Ogirisi: A New Journal of African Studies* 6 (2009): 24–39.

Cohen, David William. "The Undefining of Oral Tradition," *Ethnohistory* 36, no. 1 (1989): 9–18.

Conrad, Joseph. *Heart of Darkness* (London: Penguin Books, 2007).

Cooper, Frederick. "Conflict and Connection: Rethinking Colonial African History," *American Historical Review* 99, no. 5 (1994): 1516–1545.

Crook, Richard C. "Decolonization, the Colonial State, and Chieftaincy in the Gold Coast," *African Affairs* 85, no. 338 (1986): 75–106.

Davidson, Basil. *The Black Man's Burden: Africa and the Curse of the Nation-State* (New York: Times Books/Random House, 1992).

Decker, Stephanie. "Postcolonial Transitions in Africa: Decolonization in West Africa and Present Day South Africa," *Journal of Management Studies* 47, no. 5 (2010): 791–813.

Diamond, Stanley and Eric Wolf. *In Search of the Primitive: A Critique of Civilization* (London: Routledge, 2017).

Dijck, José van. *The Culture of Connectivity: A Critical History of Social Media* (Oxford: Oxford University Press, 2013).

Dike, Kenneth Onwuka. "African History Twenty-Five Years Ago and Today," *Journal of the Historical Society of Nigeria* 10, no. 3 (1980): 13–22.

Dike, Kenneth. *Trade and Politics in the Niger Delta, 1830–1885: An Introduction to the Economic and Political History of Nigeria* (Westport: Greenwood Press, 1981).

Dobie, Madeleine. *Trading Places: Colonization and Slavery in Eighteenth-Century French Culture* (New York: Cornell University Press, 2010).

Earle, Jonathon L. *African Intellectual History and Historiography* (Oxford: Oxford Research Encyclopedia of African History, 2018).

Eleni, Mourdoukoutas. "The Hashtag Revolution Gaining Ground," *Africa Renewal, United Nations,* accessed May 2, 2020, https://www.un.org/africarenewal/magazine/april-2018-july-2018/hashtag-revolution-gaining-ground.

Enaifoghe, Andrew Osehi. "The Decolonization of African Education and History," *African Renaissance* (1744–2532) 16, no. 1 (2019): 61–84.

Essoungou, Andre-Michel. "A Social Media Boom Begins in Africa," *Africa Renewal* 24, no. 4 (2010): 3–4.

Falola, Toyin and Christian Jennings, eds. *Africanizing Knowledge: African Studies Across the Disciplines* (London: Routledge, 2017).

Falola, Toyin and Christian Jennings, eds. *Sources and Methods in African History: Spoken, Written, Unearthed* (Rochester: University of Rochester Press, 2003).

Falola, Toyin. *Nationalism and African Intellectuals* (New York: University Rochester Press, 2004).

Gosden, Chris and Chantal Knowles. *Collecting Colonialism: Material Culture and Colonial Change* (London: Routledge, 2020).

Handlin, Oscar. *Truth in History* (London: Routledge, 2018).

Harrison, Nicholas. *Our Civilizing Mission: The Lessons of Colonial Education* (Liverpool: Liverpool University Press, 2019).

Heap, Simon. "The Nigerian National Archives, Ibadan: An Introduction for Users and a Summary of Holdings," *History in Africa* 18 (1991): 159–172.

Heleta, Savo. "Decolonizing Knowledge in South Africa: Dismantling the 'Pedagogy of Big Lies,'" *Ufahamu: A Journal of African Studies* 40, no. 2 (2018): 47–65.

Hobsbawm, Eric. "From Social History to the History of Society," *Daedalus* 100, no. 1 (1971): 20–45.

Johnson, Joseph. "Africa: Number of Internet Users in Selected Countries 2020," *Statista*, May 25, 2021, https://www.statista.com/statistics/262966/number-of-internet-users-in-selected-countries/.

Juang, Richard M. and Noelle Morrissette, eds. *Africa and the Americas: Culture, Politics, and History: A Multidisciplinary Encyclopedia, Vol. 1* (Santa Barbara: ABC-CLIO, 2008).

Kamola, Isaac A. "Pursuing Excellence in a 'World-Class African University': The Mamdani Affair and the Politics of Global Higher Education," *Journal of Higher Education in Africa* 9, no. 1–2 (2011): 147–168.

Klein, Martin A. *Slavery and Colonial Rule in French West Africa* (Cambridge: Cambridge University Press, 1998).

Lawrance, Benjamin N., Emily Lynn Osborn and Richard L. Roberts, eds. *Intermediaries, Interpreters, and Clerks: African Employees in the Making of Colonial Africa* (Madison: University of Wisconsin Press, 2006).

Livsey, Tim. "The University Age: Development and Decolonisation in Nigeria, 1930 to 1966" (PhD Diss., Birkbeck College, University of London, 2014).

Lugard, Frederick. *The Dual Mandate in British Tropical Africa* (Edinburgh: William Blackwood and Sons, 1922).

Macfarlane, David. "UCT in War over 'Bantu Education,'" *Mail & Guardian,* March 11, 2011, https://mg.co.za/article/2011-03-11-uct-in-war-over-bantu-education/.

Martin, Guy. "Africa and the Ideology of Eurafrica: Neo-Colonialism or Pan-Africanism?" *Journal of Modern African Studies* 20, no. 2 (1982): 221–238.

Mbembe, Achille Joseph. "Decolonizing the University: New Directions," *Arts and Humanities in Higher Education* 15, no. 1 (2016): 29–45.

McCall, Daniel F. *Africa in Time-Perspective, A Discussion of Historical Reconstruction from Unwritten Sources* (New York: Oxford University Press, 1969).

Msiska, Mpalive-Hangson and Paul Hyland. *Writing and Africa* (London: Routledge, 2017).

Mswazie, Jonathan and Tapiwa Mudyahoto. "Africanizing the Curriculum: An Adaptive Framework for Reforming African Education Systems," *Journal of Emerging Trends in Educational Research and Policy Studies* 4, no. 1 (2013): 170–177.

Musere, Jonathan. *Africa: The Dark Continent according to Foreigners* (Los Angeles: Ariko Publications, 2016).

Ndlovu Gatsheni, Sabelo J. "Decoloniality as the Future of Africa," *History Compass* 13, no. 10 (2015): 485–496.

Ndlovu-Gatsheni, Sabelo J. *Epistemic Freedom in Africa: Deprovincialization and Decolonization* (London: Routledge, 2018).

Negedu, Isaiah A. and Solomon O. Ojomah. "Deconstructing African History from Western Historicism," *Alternation* 23, no. 1 (2018): 302–325.

Nyamnjoh, Francis B. "Decolonizing the University in Africa," *Oxford Research Encyclopedia of Politics,* July 29, 2019, https://oxfordre.com/politics/view/10.1093/acrefore/9780190228637.001.0001/acrefore-9780190228637-e-717.

Obichere, Boniface I. "The Contribution of African Scholars and Teachers to African Studies, 1955–1975," *African Issues* 6, no. 2–3 (1976): 27–32.

Omer-Cooper, John D. "The Contribution of the University of Ibadan to the Spread of the Study and Teaching of African History within Africa," *Journal of the Historical Society of Nigeria* 10, no. 3 (1980): 23–31.

Owen, Richard, Phil Macnaghten and Jack Stilgoe. "Responsible Research and Innovation: From Science in Society to Science for Society, with Society." *Science and Public Policy* 39, no. 6 (2012): 751–760.

Oyewumi, Oyeronke. "Conceptualizing Gender: Eurocentric Foundations of Feminist Concepts and the Challenge of African Epistemologies," in Signe Anfred, Bibi Bakare-Yusuf, Edward W. Kisiang'ani, Desiree Lewis, Oyeronke Oyewumi and Filomina C. Steady, eds., *African Gender Scholarship: Concepts, Methodologies and Paradigms* (Senegal: CODESRIA, 2004): 1–8.

Perrin, Andrew. "Social Media Usage," Pew Research Center 125 (2015): 52–68.

Pihama, Leonie and Jenny Lee-Morgan. "Colonization, Education, and Indigenous Peoples," in Elizabeth Ann Mckinley and Linda Tuhiwai Smith, eds., *Handbook of Indigenous Education* (Senegal: CODESRIA, 2019), 19–27.

Rathbone, Richard. "Cultured Nations-Self-Assertion and Brokerage," in Pailo Fernando de Moraes Farias and Karin Barber, eds., *Early Cultural Nationalism in West Africa* (Birmingham: University of Birmingham, 1990).

Shizha, Edward. "Are we There Yet? Theorizing a Decolonizing Science Education for Development in Africa," in Ali A. Abdi, ed., *Decolonizing Philosophies of Education* (Rotterdam: Sense Publishers, 2012), 163–176.

Small, Stephen. "Slavery, Colonialism and their Legacy in the Eurocentric University," *Human Architecture: Journal of the Sociology of Self-Knowledge* 10, no. 1 (2012): 69–80.

Smith, Andrew W. M. "Pan-Africanism and Decolonization: Between the Universal and the Particular," in Reiland Rabaka, ed., *Routledge Handbook of Pan-Africanism* (London: Routledge, 2020), 112–124.

Statista. "Most Popular Social Networks Worldwide as of January 2022, Ranked by Number of Monthly Active Users," *Statista Research Department,* accessed May 1, 2022, https://www.statista.com/statistics/272014/global-social-networks-ranked-by-number-of-users/.

Sturm, Christian and Hossam Amer. "The Effects of (Social) Media on Revolutions—Perspectives from Egypt and the Arab Spring," in Masaaki Kurosu, ed., *Human-Computer Interaction: Users and Contexts of Use* (Berlin: Springer, 2013), 352–358.

Tamarkin, Mordechai. *The Making of Zimbabwe: Decolonization in Regional and International Politics* (London: Routledge, 2012).

Taylor, Ian and Paul Williams. *Africa in International Politics: External Involvement on the Continent* (London: Routledge, 2004).

Tibebu, Teshale. *Hegel and the Third World: The Making of Eurocentrism in World History* (New York: Syracuse University Press, 2011).

Tsheola, Johannes. "Trade Regionalism, Decolonization-Bordering and the New Partnership for Africa's Development," *China-USA Business Review* 11, no. 8 (2012): 1051–1068.

Vansina, Jan. *Oral Tradition: A Study in Historical Methodology (London: Heinemann Educational Books, 1968).*

Vysotskaia, N. I. and Arlo Schultz. "The Struggle of the African Peoples against Neocolonialism," *International Journal of Politics* 6, no. 4 (1976–77): 12–49.

Walters, Ronald W. *Pan Africanism in the African Diaspora: An Analysis of Modern Afrocentric Political Movements* (Detroit: Wayne State University Press, 1997).

Wansbrough, John. "The Decolonization of North African History," *The Journal of African History* 9, no. 4 (1968): 643–650.

Were, Anzetse. *Debt Trap? Chinese Loans and Africas Development Options* (Johannesburg: South African Institute of International Affairs, 2018), 3–12.

Windel, Aaron. "British Colonial Education in Africa: Policy and Practice in the Era of Trusteeship," *History Compass* 7, no. 1 (2009): 1–21.

Woldegiorgis, Emnet Tadesse and Martin Doevenspeck. "The Changing Role of Higher Education in Africa: A Historical Reflection," *Higher Education Studies* 3, no. 6 (2013): 35–45.

Yusuf, Folashade. "The Role of Archives in National Development: National Archives of Nigerian Perspective," *International Journal of Economic Development Research and Investment* 4, no. 2 (2013): 19–24.

Zeleza, Paul T. Banishing the Silences: *Towards the Globalization of African History* (Maputo: CODESRIA, 2005).

CARL SCHLETTWEIN LECTURES

The distinguished lecture of the Centre for African Studies Basel is held in remembrance of Dr h.c. Carl Schlettwein, who played an important part in the development of African Studies at Basel and in the establishment of the Centre. His moral support was supplemented by the generous and farsighted assistance he gave to these activities. Carl Schlettwein was born in Mecklenburg in 1925 and emigrated to South Africa in 1952. Until 1963 he lived in South West Africa, the former German colony that was then under South African administration. When he married Daniela Gsell he moved to Basel. In 1971 Schlettwein founded the Basler Afrika Bibliographien (BAB) as a library and publishing house in order to allow international institutions to access bibliographic information on South West Africa (Namibia). Accordingly, he published the first national bibliography on this African country. Through these activities the BAB contributed to documenting and researching a nation with a particularly difficult history. Other publications dealt with historical, literary and geo-methodological topics, and included titles on Swiss-African relations. From an individualistic private initiative, the BAB developed into an institution open to the public and became a cornerstone of the Centre for African Studies Basel. As the Namibia Resource Centre—Southern Africa Library the institution is of world-wide importance. The Carl Schlettwein Foundation, which was founded in 1994, runs the

BAB and supports students and projects in Namibia as well as in other Southern African countries. In 2001, the Carl Schlettwein Foundation funded the establishment of the Chair of African History, providing the basis for today's professorship in African History and the African Studies programme at the University of Basel. The Foundation works closely with the Centre for African Studies Basel to provide support for teaching and research and in 2016 it enabled the Centre to establish a position on Namibian and Southern African Studies. The University of Basel honoured Carl Schlettwein with an honorary doctorate in 1997.